A World to Share

By Dean Walley

Illustrated by Jay Johnson

♛ Hallmark Crown Editions

There is a world to share.....

.....a world as fresh as morning

.....as bright as a dream

of sunlight on wide water.....

.....as peaceful as a prayer.

We can walk there together

....away from the cities....

....toward a

green forest, silently awaiting us....

....full of secret places

no one has seen before....

....and we can find a morning world

to share.... a world refreshed by night

....awakened by the sun.

It is the springtime of the day

and promises unfold around us....

....opening flowers, budding trees....

....the first bird songs

of morning.

The morning is like the beginning

of friendship....unsure, hesitant, expectant.

First light out of darkness....

....hope for what lies ahead....

....JOY.

And we can exult in the world we share.

We see trees writing poems against the sky.

The wind song is our music.

The dawning of this beautiful day

is etched on our hearts....

.....as unforgettable

as the beginning of friendship.

Walking through the green wood, we see

a deer....

....frozen in a moment

that seems forever....

....then he leaps away....

....a streak of brown

disappearing in the leaves.

The sight of him is like the first sight

of a new friend....

....a friend who is timid and shy

....who bolts away suddenly,

leaving a sense of wonder....

....a desire to meet again.

Now a stream....

....a crystal trail

....leads us into the wilderness

....into ourselves.

And we follow the bright waters wherever

they lead....

....beyond the morning world

....to a place where the sun

is at its zenith....

....to the summer of the day.
The world is warm around us. The tears
of night and the haze and uncertainty
of morning disappear in this strong,
secure noontime we share....

....and everywhere

glows the sun.

Its rays dance on the rippled waters.

Its warmth mingles with the wind.

Its strong fingers reach

into the cool earth....

....nourishing wild flowers

and lacy ferns.

It speaks to the sleeping seeds

and coaxes them to life.

The forest pays tribute to the sun

....birds sing of its glory

....trees reach their limbs skyward

in praise.

And the good, brown earth smiles a warm,

contented smile....

Deep in the heart of the day, the sun....

....and blue heaven itself....

seem to bend to us, knowing

we cannot climb.

It is a golden world we share.

The still waters are burnished with gold....

....they shimmer and gleam

when the wind passes by.

The dark places are made light....

...even the dark places

of our hearts.

The hidden wonders are revealed

and all the mysteries are solved.

It is like the summer of friendship
....the time when shyness is
forgotten and trust is forged....strong
and enduring.

Time when all is revealed....and accepted.

Glad-hearted time of the strong handclasp

and merry laughter....

.....time we share.

We follow the sun now....out of the
tangle of trees and vines....into an open
place....a golden field in the afternoon.

It is a drowsy place, day-dreaming
in the lazy afternoon. A place where we
can pause and talk....and share our dreams.

Time loses its power over us.

We spend moments here....or are they
hours? Time isn't measured....

....except in our hearts.

And we walk on, refreshed, back into
the forest. It grows darker now. And the
moving shadows of leaves gently blend
....recalling the combining patterns
of our lives.

We share the world at twilight.

It is the autumn of the day....

.....the shadow time.

The sun is larger than before....

.....but kinder, less intense

.....a mellow disc of orange

light

.....falling through the mountain peaks

and turning the forest to flame

.....falling somewhere far away

and summoning up layers of pink

and golden clouds to reflect

its farewell....

.....setting in splendor....

.....rising in another land

to start the miracle of another day.

We are alone now in the half-light....

....in the place of shadows.

The old mysteries return to us.

It is time to wait

for that first star of evening....

....time to listen

to our memories.

As the world around us

begins to fade from view,

we can hear the sounds of evening....

....sounds of the wind,

brushing branch to branch,

rippling a pool of water,

bending grasses

to kiss the earth....

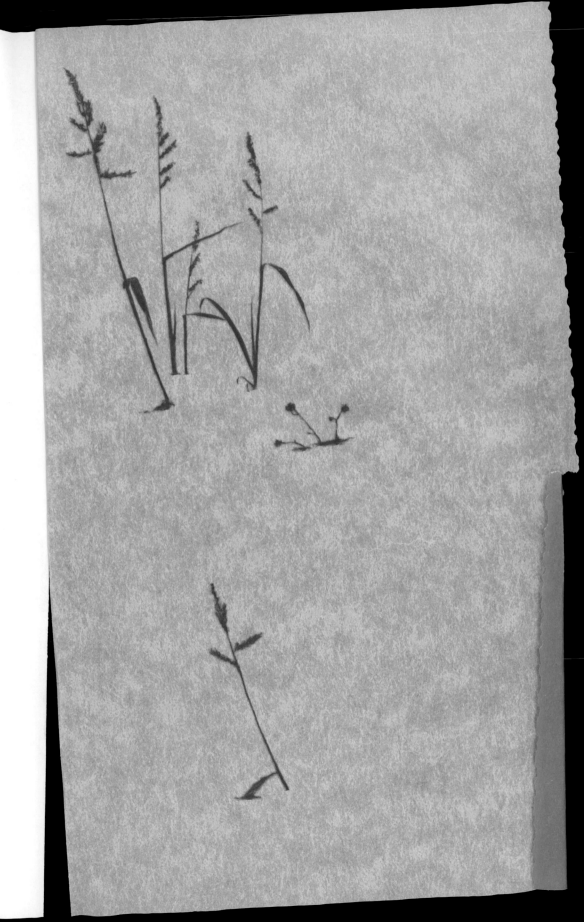

....sounds of all the creatures

of the forest

preparing for night....

....the squirrels and the birds....

....the elusive sounds of unseen

animals who dart away

when we are near....

....the sounds of silence....

....rarest sounds of all.

For when we pause and listen

with an inner stillness....

....when the wind calms

and no birds call....

....the sounds of silence can be heard

....sometimes more clearly than the fury

of a storm.

We linger here....in the winter

of the day.

The forest is dark around us,

but we are not afraid....

....for now there is a new world above us

....one more for us to share.

And we are filled up and content
with the day....

for the forest has spoken to us
and the wild birds have taught us.

We have traveled with the sun
and the wind....

....and now it is good to rest.

The stars are so very still tonight.

....their pure light is reassuring....

....eternal.

And the moon is near to us....

....friendly.

It is looking at itself

in lakes and rivers

all over the world....

....smiling back at itself

in the night.

The stars...

...the moon...

...and our hearts

are at peace.

In the darkness....looking up

at the grandeur of the universe....our world

seems so very small. Yet it seems,

more than ever,

one world.

We no longer hear the wind curling

around us....we are one with the wind.

And all the trees in the forest,

in the world, are as one tree....to give us

shade by day and shelter by night.

And all the streams are as one stream,

....reaching to the same sea....

....and you and I are one....

....one with all men everywhere.

Laughing as one, crying as one....

....living as one as we face the common

mystery.

....walking together in perfect harmony

....surrounded by the greater

harmony....

....the infinite wonder....

....of a world we share.

This book was designed and illustrated by Jay Johnson.
The artist made his own color separations
and closely supervised the printing for utmost accuracy of reproduction.
The type is set in Firenze, a typeface designed
exclusively for Hallmark by Hermann Zapf.
The paper is Hallclear, White Imitation Parchment
and Ivory Fiesta Parchment.
The cover is bound with imported natural Seta
silk book cloth and Torino paper.